CALIFORNIA
THE GOLDEN STATE

Written, Designed and Edited
By
Randy Collings

Published By
ADAM RANDOLPH COLLINGS
incorporated

Box 8658 Holiday Station, Anaheim, California 92802

This book was printed by Frye and Smith Lithograph Company, Costa Mesa, California, from Litho Film prepared by Frye and Smith, San Diego, California.

Cover: Symbol of romantic Spanish California, beautiful Mission Santa
　　　Barbara has served the faithful since 1815 (photograph by Craig Aurness).
Title Page: Each spring the poppy, California's state flower, sets hillsides
　　　ablaze with a sunshine brilliance all its own (photograph by Bill Ross).
Opening Spreads in order: Spectacular Big Sur (photograph by James
　　　Randklev). Primeval grove in Redwood National Park (photograph by
　　　Roy Murphy). 14,495 foot Mt. Whitney towers above the Alabama
　　　Hills (photograph by Roy Murphy).
This Page: ''King of the Missions'' San Luis Rey de Francia in Oceanside,
　　　near San Diego.
Last Page: Splendid Yosemite Falls, second highest cataract in the world
　　　(photograph by Ed Cooper).
Back Cover: Magnificent Yosemite Valley (photograph by William Neill).

CALIFORNIA

THE GOLDEN STATE

DISCOVERY: September 28, 1542 at Point Loma in San Diego, by Juan Rodriguez Cabrillo, a Portuguese maritimer sailing under the flag of Spain.

SETTLED: Beginning at San Diego in 1769 by Captain Gaspar de Portola and Father Junipero Serra (founder of the California Mission Chain).

ADMISSION TO
THE UNION: September 9, 1850, as the 31st State.

CAPITOL: Sacramento

MAJOR CITIES: Los Angeles • San Diego • San Francisco

SIZE: 158,693 square miles; third largest state in the union; with a population approaching 24,000,000.

DESCRIPTION: 1,264 miles of coastline fronting on the Pacific Ocean. Northern realms receive an annual rainfall of some 110 inches, while southern environs average less than 10 inches of precipitation a year.

Two major mountain systems, the Sierra Nevada and Coast Range, running north and south, merge with the Tehachapis, running east and west, in the south and the Cascade Range in the north, to create the vast Central Valley of California's interior.

The San Joaquin and Sacramento river systems drain into San Francisco's immense bay. Elsewhere, San Diego's natural harbor is the State's only other bay of any consequence, although the man-made port of Los Angeles, is by far the most important to the State's economy.

Beyond the Sierra Nevada and Southern California's extensive Los Angeles Basin lies the arid Colorado and Mojave Deserts.

MARK MILLER

CALIFORNIA
THE GOLDEN STATE

Picture in your mind a land of infinite beauty and endless variety; a country where snow covered mountains tower above green, undulating hills, creating alpine environs on the edge of subtropic landscapes. A gentle place, where the climate is equable and the living comfortable. Where the palaces of the affluent and the bungalows of the modest grace a common countryside. Where supercities are subdued by the blessings of spaciousness and geographic diversity.

Imagine a place a place where genius and talent are abundant and overnight success is commonplace. A mecca for the aggressive and the laid back. Where desert oasis and white sand beaches invite the every whim of the hedonist as they nurture the activities of the more temperate.

In this beautiful volume of color photography and text we invite you to explore the romance and mystery of this most exceptional of countries - home of the purveyors of pleasure - birthplace of the world's most sought after lifestyle - CALIFORNIA.

UTTA KARIN HARRISON

BILL ROSS

THE SOUTH COAST

California's South Coast begins somewhere along Big Sur where, after a hundred miles of mountains tumbling into the sea, the landscape is suddenly subdued by a less precipitous coastline. Vast expanses of sandy beach have been formed as the more gently sloping coastal shelf reaches out into mother ocean's embrace. Sheltered harbors (mostly man-made) offer safe anchorage for thousands of pleasure crafts, while extensive salt water estuaries provide sanctuary for marine wildlife.

Further south the awesome Los Angeles basin, home of America's second largest community, spills its chrome and steel metropolis out over the very edge of the continent; giving rise to a society nourished by sun, sand, and surf. This is the buccolic California of popular notion - a realm of balmy sea breezes, palm studded suburbs, exotic automobiles, and beautiful people.

The mystique of LA pours across political boundaries to neighboring Orange County, where countless manufacturing and aerospace giants have taken up residence in the shadow of Walt Disney's Anaheim kingdom. Once a rural citrus producing valley, Orange County has since been appraised as perhaps the nation's single most valuable piece of real estate.

Beyond a thousand hills and pine covered summits lies California's second most populous community - San Diego. In 1542 a Spanish galleon, commandeered by Captain Juan Rodriguez Cabrillo, sailed into this "most perfect harbor" and claimed the newfound frontier for the Spanish Crown. They bestowed upon their discovery the most unusual name of CALIFORNIA, an island spoken of in a popular novel embellishing knighthood and chivalry.

Centuries of Spanish colonization efforts would follow. To this day the golden coast of Southern California retains a certain Latin ambiance and charm unique to itself.

ROY MURPHY

At California's birthplace humble adobe dwellings and mission bell towers are dwarfed by San Diego's superstructures (right). Preserving her rich Spanish heritage has succeeded in bestowing upon this modern 21st Century prototype community an element of charm and tranquility not found elsewhere in cities of comparable size. Case in point is the beautiful Mission San Diego de Alcala (above) founded in 1769 by Franciscan padre Junipero Serra. Today, fully restored, this primitive yet graceful structure shares a common hillside with red-tile roofed condominiums and business parks.

TONY KAWAHIMA

America's most equable climate produces a commercial flower crop in San Diego of more than 50 colorful and fragrant tons each year (above).

Boasting the finest recreational and entertainment facilities in the Country, Mission Bay, one of this city's most outstanding achievements, encompasses more than 4,600 master-planned acres of aquatic playground. Crowning jewel of this multi-million dollar development is the Sea World theme park (above right), where killer whales and dolphins provide outstanding family entertainment as well as close-at-hand observation for advanced marine studies.

Across town stretches exotic Balboa Park, home of the largest and most sophisticated zoological park in the world (right). Larger collections of rare wildlife from around the world roam free in the San Diego Zoo's Wild Animal Park at nearby Escondido.

BILL ROSS

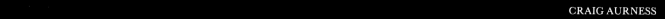

"The Happiest Place on Earth," Disneyland (left and below) plays host to more than 11 million guests annually. Each of its seven schematic "lands" offers unique and unrivaled adventures engineered and designed by Disney's ever-innovative "imagineers." Walt accurately predicted that his Anaheim theme park would never be complete "as long as there was imagination left in the world." Today his Magic Kingdom continues to expand and grow more beautiful under a master plan that entices guests with new themed attractions and shows debuting each year.

Nearby, Knott's Berry Farm (right), oldest theme park in America, abounds in rollicking wild west adventures, thrill rides, outstanding giftshops and fine dining.

CRAIG AURNESS

DON TORMEY

MARK MILLER

STEVE SAKAMOTO

UTTA KARIN HARRISON

AMERICAN STOCK PHOTO

MARK MILLER

Southern California is famous for its excellent white sand beaches and perennial sunshine. Here surfers and sunworshippers congregate year-round to partake of the pleasures of life on the coast.

At Newport Harbor, in Orange County, ornate and historic Balboa Pavillion (above), built in 1905, serves as recreational epicenter for the world's busiest small craft harbor.

CRAIG AURNESS

A nation's window into the future, Los Angeles (left and page 15) has emerged from obscurity to assume her role as the single most important metropolis west of the Hudson River. A city of dreamers and achievers, LA is the world's trendsetter in most every field imaginable.

Home of Hollywood, "Entertainment Capitol of the World", Los Angeles also features such outstanding attractions as the regal "Queen Mary" (below left) at permanent birth in Long Beach, an exciting "behind-the-scenes" tour of the world's largest motion picture studio in Universal City, and Magic Mountain - one of the country's finest amusement parks.

PIERRE KOPP

Vertical, timbered walls and isolated peaks bisect and beautify Southern California's largely urban landscape, sheltering her temperate coastal valleys and catching, for that coast, the precipitation of each Pacific storm that passes through.

At an elevation exceeding 11,000 feet, Mount San Gorgonio (right) stands as the South Coast's highest summit. Beyond Mount San Jacinto, in the beautiful Anza Valley (below) and along the foothills of the San Gabriel Mountains (left) spectacular displays of wild flowers paint the slopes following Southern California's rainy season.

Tenth of the 21 missions of Old California, founded in 1786 and named in honor of the Roman virgin who was beheaded by her pagan father for having embraced Christianity, Santa Barbara today remains the West Coast's finest example of a Colonial Spanish community.

Romantically situated between the Pacific's sweeping coastline and the gentle, wooded slopes of the Santa Ynez Mountains, Santa Barbara, with its omnipresent Spanish-Moorish architecture, epitomizes the Southern California of legend. Master storytellers have since embellished these settings in tales such as that of Zorro, early California's Robin Hood who stoled from the wealthy rancheros to give to the impoverished peons.

Historical center for a heirarchy of Spanish landbarons and focal point for missionary activities along the coast, Santa Barbara has indeed a rich heritage to impart upon modern-day Californians.

The Classical Spanish Mission (this page) that graces this community was first constructed in 1794. Its ornate facade and belltowers as seen today, were completed in 1815 and later renovated in 1950. Reflective of the remarkable faith and devotion of a handful of Franciscans who, with nothing more than primitive tools and unskilled Indian labor, managed to raise an ediface of such grandeur in the midst of a wilderness virtually at the very end of the earth, causes those of us born in an era of comfort and technology to marvel.

Beyond the beaches and marina of Santa Barbara lie the Channel Islands, final resting place of California's discoverer, Captain Juan Rodriguez Cabrillo, and newest addition to America's National Park System.

On a mountaintop overlooking the Pacific at San Simeon, rises the magnificent estate of publishing giant William Randolph Hearst. Crowning "the enchanted hill" stands what has since become known as Heart's Castle, the most opulent home in America. Today, preserved by the California State Park System, the 146 room "house" contains priceless art treasures from the Old World. Open to public inspection, the Castle hosts an unending stream of visitors from the moment that it opens each morning until it closes its doors in the late afternoon.

Just north of Santa Barbara, Scandinavian charm permeates the air at Solvang (far right and above far right) where a significant Danish population maintain, to the delight of Californians, the traditional architecture, foods, and folk festivals of their homeland.

At Estero Bay (right), the 576 foot high volcanic formation of Morro Rock greets travelers as a familiar landmark along a picturesque coast. Here it was that California's first exploring party camped back in 1769.

Beyond San Simeon, the shoreline takes on a perpendicular dimension, as mountain ramparts push into the sea at Big Sur (above).

KEN RAVEILL

CRAIG AURNESS

ED COOPER

DESERT COUNTRY

In ancient times much of California's eastern frontier lay beneath the waters of a vast inland sea. Forests of primeval palm trees grew along its shores. A temperate climate nurtured an abundance of flora and fauna.

With the birth of the mighty Sierra Nevada mountain range, life-giving precipitation from the Pacific was virtually cutoff. Aided by a universal warming trend, extensive grasslands were transformed into the forboding, yet strikingly beautiful desert landscape that we see today.

Actually two separate geographic entities, the Mojave and Colorado Deserts together encompass nearly one-fifth of California's total landmass. As might be expected, the ever ingenious Californians have transformed much of this "wasteland" into posh resorts and rich farmlands.

ROY MURPHY

Ominous Death Valley (photographs these pages) perhaps best symbolizes the harsh desert world of the Mojave. Named by an ill-fated emmigrant train seeking speedier access to the gold fields in 1849, the absolute desolation of this region is not easily comprehended by those who marvel at the Valley's eerie landscape from automobiles and linger for evenings around the swimming pool at posh Furnace Creek Resort.

Today a national monument, this 140 mile long sink between the Panamint and Amargosa Ranges is one of the hottest and driest places on earth. Shifting sand dunes and stark geologic formations such as Zabriski Point (below) or Tin Mountain (left) add to the beauty of this prehistoric wilderness.

At 282 feet below sea level, Badwater (right), in Death Valley, is the lowest elevation of any location within the United States.

AMERICAN STOCK PHOTO

ROY MURPHY

ROY MURPHY

Joshua Tree National Monument (above) and ultra scenic Redrock Canyon (left) are popular sites for desert recreation and contemplation. Today their settings are familiar to millions as the location of many motion picture and television productions.

Named by early Mormon settlers, the Joshua Tree itself is a curious plant, related to the lily family, yet growing up to 50 feet in height and reportedly living as long as two hundred years.

MARK MILLER

CRAIG AURNESS

Chic Palm Springs, once a tiny desert oasis, has since, through the ingeniuty and engineering feats of man, become a world renowned resort.

LA's playground, the dazzling verdure of a city carpeted in golf fairways, dotted with spas and pools and divided by groves of date palms, is set off strikingly against the pale, burnished earth tones of the Colorado desert.

Fast cars, resident celebrities, and incomparable dining and nightclub offerings, all basking beneath a warm, dry climate and clear blue sky, make of the Springs an environ unique in and of itself. Each year winter-weary snowbirds retreat to this sun-bathed paradise to relax and play.

38   DESERT COUNTRY

CHUCK O'REAR

MARK MILLER

MARK MILLER

CRAIG AURNESS

THE SIERRA NEVADA

Most striking geologic feature of the Golden State is a 400 mile long block of granite known as the Sierra Nevada Range. Rising at vertical angles, these mighty mountains shelter California's temperate coastal regions from the searing heat of the great deserts beyond. Watershed from an annual snowfall that frequently exceeds 400 inches, provides irrigation for America's most productive agricultural region, while at the same time accommodating the millions who have come to settle in arid Southern California.

Rich timberlands and unparalleled mountain scenery form a spectacular backdrop for El Dorado. Hamlets and Ghost Towns bestow upon this rugged region an aura of fantasy, conjuring up recollections of gold strikes and silver booms. Here it was that California yielded a multi-billion dollar harvest of gold bullion to forty-niners lucky enough to reach the Sierra before the world came pouring in.

While the spread of civilization, initiated by the Gold Rush, has since procluded the perpetuation of much of the West Coast's once abundant wildlife population, this giant range of mountains affords a sanctuary wherein great bears still roam the woods, and herds of deer browse peacefully in high mountain meadows.

Along the gently sloping western face of the Sierra stand prehistoric groves of ancient Sequoias. These hugh trees, towering hundreds of feet above the floor of the forest, constitute the largest living things on earth.

To preserve the many unique features of California's High Sierra, John Muir, America's most beloved naturalist, initiated conservation efforts that have since resulted in the formation of three national parks and countless reserves. Today this rich natural heritage promises urban-weary man a legacy of unspoiled wilderness in which to calm his spirit and heal his soul.

BILL ROSS

Gold Rush charm in Auburn (this page) reminiscent of the New England villages from which many of her first settlers came. Since the days of forty-nine this picturesque community, nestled in the foothills of the High Sierra, remains a viable entity. Minutes from Sacramento, Auburn serves as a center of commerce for much of the historic 'Mother Lode' country.

ED COOPER

Shrine of the Sierra, Yosemite Valley with its towering peaks, lacy waterfalls, and park-like meadows is among the world's most beautiful garden spots. Here powerful Yosemite Falls (right) plummets over the rim of the valley in a drop of 2,425 feet, making it the second highest waterfall in the world. Across the chasm beautiful Bridal Veil Falls (below right) pours into the mountain throneroom from high country snowfields beyond.

Vernal Falls' mist trail (below) is a popular hiking destination for many Yosemite visitors.

PAT O'HARA

ED COOPER

ED COOPER

EMIL FORLER

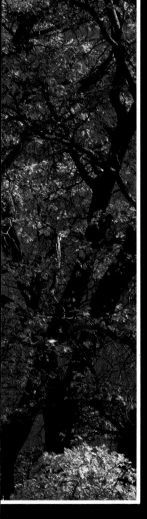

Autumn adds a sharp crispness to the air and a splash of color to the many world famous monoliths of Yosemite National Park. The Sentinal (left) guardian of the Valley, El Capitan (below) and Half Dome (below left) are among the most prominent features of this glaciated labyrinth.

ED COOPER

In winter the glory of Yosemite is shrouded beneath a mantle of white. El Capitan (above), takes on a cold, steel blue appearance. The Grand Old Ahwahnee Hotel (far right) beckons chilled mountaineers to step inside and warm themselves by the hearth of her great stone fireplace.

Further south, in Sequoia National Park, magnificent General Sherman, at 275 feet in height and 40 feet in diameter, stands like a king, reportedly the largest living thing on earth, cloaked in white.

Winter sport enthusiasts take to the mountains en mass to indulge in cross country ski expeditions and downhill slalom competitions at any one of a number of outstanding Sierra resorts.

ROY MURPHY

EMIL FORLER

EMIL FORLER

DAVE GRABER

PAT O'HARA

ED COOPER

EMIL FORLER

Spring comes late to the High Sierra. Green grass and tiny alpine blossoms blanket Toulomne Meadows (far left), snow-fed rivers and falls swell to overflowing (above left), great bears (above far left) awake from their winter slumber (California bears apparently find California sunshine as intoxicating as do we humans. Not true hibernators, they are often seen ambling about the snowdrifts foraging and playing in the warm sunshine), and backpackers set out for high adventure. Unique features such as the Devil's Postpile (left) are popular destinations.

ED COOPER

CRAIG AURNESS

CRAIG AURNESS

ED COOPER

Gem of the Sierra, Lake Tahoe, with its crystal blue waters and pine-clad shores, forms a picture postcard setting for distinctive mountain homes and resorts.

Formed at the end of the last great Ice Age by melting glaciers, Tahoe's 12 mile wide expanse sits like a giant bowl amidst rugged peaks, many towering in excess of 10,000 feet above the Nevada desert.

Scenic Highway 395 skirts the eastern flank of the mighty Sierra, affording spectacular vistas of mountain citadels, pine and aspen forests, and desert wilderness.

Not far from Virginia City, site of the famous Comstock Lode, lies Bodie (next page) a one-time boomtown of more than 10,000 gold seekers. Today a ghost town, its buildings and atmosphere are preserved as a State Historic Park.

THE SIERRA NEVADA 53

ED COOPER

Bridgeport (below), with its Victorian Courthouse, circa 1880, and tourist trade, serves as gateway to some of the finest fishing and hunting grounds in the state.

Silent Mono Lake (right), an inland sea dotted with islands of volcanic origin, is so alkaline that only tiny brine shrimp inhabit its waters.

Southernmost peak of the Sierra, stately Mount Whitney (below right), near Bishop, at 14,495 feet is the highest summit in the continental United States.

ED COOPER

THE CENTRAL VALLEY

Although generally associated with glamorous beaches and urban sprawl, it is a lesser known fact that California is the agricultural capital of the nation. Here farm towns and rural villages far outnumber the super cities for which the state has become famous. At the heart of the nation's richest farming region is the extensive 465 mile long Central Valley, the largest such open basin in the world. Runoff from the High Sierras feed into the Valley's two great river systems, the Sacramento and the San Joaquin, while numerous reservoirs, canals, and pumping stations redirect precious watershed into the more arid reaches of the state, thus extending even further the vastness of this agricultural empire.

Rich soil and a long growing season pay off for California's 63,000 farmers in multi billion dollar harvests annually.

The greatest variety of fresh fruit, vegetables, grains, meat, and poultry available anywhere in the world are produced on some 36 million acres of rich California farm and dairylands, providing one out of every three jobs for California workers and supplying about one quarter of the nation's table food.

CHUCK O'REAR

CHUCK O'REAR

Beautiful California-style plantations have grown up around the state's cotton raising industry, while more than 200 other crops, including everything from tomatoes and melons to almonds and rice, bring the annual harvest to ten figure numbers.

In surrounding areas rolling hills undisturbed by the plow provide miles of rambling rangeland for cattle.

Capitol City of the Golden State, Sacramento (next page) began as one man's kingdom back in 1839. Self-styled Swiss entrepreneur Johann August Sutter petitioned for and received from the Mexican government a land grant upon which to lay the foundations of an empire.

ED COOPER

CALIFORNIA REPUBLIC

Those foundations are still visible today at Sutter's Fort State Historic Park (below and below right), where costumed employees relate to wide-eyed visitors the story of the Americanization of El Dorado.

Renovated at a cost of over 60 million dollars, California's beautiful Capitol Building (right) and nearby restored Old Sacramento (far right) contrast sharply with the predominately Spanish architecture of early California, suggesting the change of power that began to take place here in this great Valley, just prior to the Gold Rush.

CHRISTOPHER SPRINGMANN

CRAIG AURNESS

CRAIG AURNESS

CRAIG AURNESS

TOM TRACY

THE NORTH COAST

Once a mere cluster of adobe huts, dwarfed by a bay "large enough to hold all the navys of Europe," as one of Portola's men described it, San Francisco, gateway to El Dorado, has since become one of the world's truly great cities. Through her golden gate flowed the largest migration of people the world has ever seen. From all corners of the globe they poured into the sanctity of California's fertile valleys - willingly investing their lives and fortunes, entrusting her with their hopes and dreams, and believing in her promise to reward their ambitions with abundance.

It is therefore the personality as much as the geography of fabled San Francisco that sets it apart as one of the world's finest. Gleaning the best from all cultures she has become an international mosaic in the very sense of the word - truly cosmopolitan.

Unlike the mediterranean landscape of the South Coast, California's northern shoreline remains verdant all year, frequently shrouded in morning and evening fog banks. Such a damp, misty environment has given rise to jungle-like rain forests wherein stand groves of ancient towering redwoods. Native to the area, these giant prehistoric trees are found nowhere else in all the world. Here they are protected in National and State Parks that stretch from the Central Coast to the Oregon border.

Fishing villages and lumber towns, reminiscent of New England's quaint settlements, draw vacationers eager to slip into a leisurely paced environment. Although the chill of the Pacific here discourages surfing and bathing, the scenic beauty of northern beaches invite hikers and browsers to examine her grand forests and wave-battered bluffs.

JIM BLANK

CRAIG AURNESS

"Everyone's favorite city," San Francisco's charm is sensed best perhaps at dusk on Fisherman's Wharf, or while riding a cable car down California Avenue as gusty crisp sea breezes muss one's hair and bring a spontaneous smile to the face - or then again perhaps as one whiles away a sunny afternoon in colorful Golden Gate Park.

CRAIG AURNESS

Romantic Carmel and Monterey (right) play host to more honeymooners then perhaps any other stretch of geography upon the face of the earth.

From Mission San Carlos Borromeo (below) Father Junipero Serra administered his conversion and colonization efforts.

At Colton Hall in Monterey (below right) the foundling Yankee government setup operations in 1849 from which the formation of America's 31st State was initiated.

In and around Napa and Sonoma is the heartland of California's famous winemaking industry. Here a perfect blend of the proper climate and rich soil produce some of the world's finest grapes. Amidst nearly 40,000 acres of vineyards stand some 50 wineries, most of which offer tours of their cellars and a sampling of their product.

CRAIG AURNESS

CRAIG AURNESS

In 1812 the Russians came to find an empire of their own based upon the marketability of sea otter pelts. Setting up operations at Fort Ross (above) and aided by Yankee entrepreneurs sailing in from New England they proceeded to hunt the curious little creatures into oblivion. Since protected, the sea otter has made a dramatic comeback and is now frequently spotted along much of California's north coast.

Redwood Country (right), makings for a capitalist's empire, attracted men such as lumber baron William Carson to California's timber rich north country. His elaborate gothic mansion is preserved today as a community heirloom in the port city of Eureka.

On the westernmost promontory of the continental United States stands picturesque Mendocino (above). In the heart of Redwood Country, its headlands are forested with ancient trees and colorful rhododendron. Deer and Roosevelt Elk (right) are a familiar site along many of the area's beaches.

ROY MURPHY

CASCADE WILDERNESS

Anciently a region of much volcanic activity, today California's northeast corner stands out as a little known region of remarkable beauty. Two magnificent extinct volcanoes, Mt. Lassen (this page) and Mt. Shasta (next page) (the latter being visible for over 100 miles), highlight the landscape, giving it much the appearance of South America's Chilean coast. Alpine landscapes reminiscent of the High Sierras together with prairie-like lowlands and hidden valleys remain wild and undeveloped.

For centuries, this country belonged to the Pauite, Pit, and Modoc Indians. Today their names remain as does the untamed nature of the land itself, appearing much as it did before the advent of the ''white man.''

ED COOPER

Crowning glory of California's northern wilderness 14,162 foot Mt. Shasta looms in icy grandeur above acres of rich timberlands. Here hearty lumberjacks still practice their trade - carefully managing forest "farmlands" so as to yield a steady flow of papergoods, building materials and a myriad of other products while at the same time preserving the delicate balance of the forest ecosystem.

THE END

ADAM RANDOLPH COLLINGS
incorporated